Never Wrestle with Pigs

Never Wrestle with Pigs

A Survival Guide for Dealing with Difficult Personalities

L. LAVON GRAY, PHD

Creative Bread

Hattiesburg, Mississippi

Printed in United States of America

ISBN: 978-0-578-22415-2

CONTENTS

To my AMAZING family...

My beautiful wife – Wendy
My daughters – Kayla, Lizzie and Katibeth
My sons-in-law – Chris and Tyler
and
My grandsons – Grayson and Henry

Thank you for extending to me more love, joy and grace
than any man deserves.

*"So now faith, hope, and love abide, these three;
but the greatest of these is love."*
1 Corinthians 13:13

One

PIGS EVERYWHERE

I learned a long time ago to never wrestle with a pig.
You both get dirty and the pig likes it.
— George Benard Shaw

For years I had a recurring dream. I'd crawl out of bed, put on my best suit and tie, climb into my truck and drive to the office…and that's when it got fun. With zero fear I'd kick open the door to my boss's office, take out my phone, shove it in his face, then smiling profusely push the play-button filling the room with the musical strains of the Johnny Paycheck standard, "Take this job and shove it, I ain't working here no more!" Oh, what joy!

Then I'd wake-up with an overwhelming sense of horror realizing it was only a dream.

I still worked at the same place…

with the same people…

facing the same problems…

in the same toxic work environment…

with no escape in sight.

This wasn't a dream; it was a nightmare!

If you've experienced something similar, you're not alone. Employees across the country are fed up and bailing at record numbers. *Gallup* indicates that 51 percent of U.S. employees are actively searching for new jobs. (Gallup 2018) This means over half of your employees are looking for an opportunity to head towards the exit. They're unhappy, disengaged, and under-productive. They show up for work in body only, simply treading water until their Johnny Paycheck moment is right. And when it is, they'll be gone!

There are numerous factors contributing to the epidemic level of job dissatisfaction in the U.S. (i.e., under-compensation, heavy workloads, life/work balance), but one of the primary culprits is workplace conflict. Employees are simply struggling to get along with each another. *Linked-In* confirmed this when they analyzed corporate skill shortages across 100 major U.S. cities. According to CEO Jeff Weiner, their research identified interpersonal skills as the largest area of "skill imbalance." More specifically, most U.S. workers can't get along with others. (Umoh 2018) This contributes to corporate cultures defined by poor communication, organizational silos and interpersonal conflict, all of which ultimately lead to high employee attrition.

Welcome to the Conflict Pigpen

Workplace conflict is engulfing your teams and it's costing your business a lot of money. In fact, the average employee wastes 2.8 hours every week dealing with conflict. These lost hours are filled with toxic activities such as gossip, employee gripe sessions, secret meetings and emotional meltdowns. The impact on the bottom line is staggering, costing U.S. employers $359 billion a year in paid hours. (CPP 2018) Let's bring that number a little closer to home.

If your employees are paid an average of $18 per hour, workplace conflict is costing your business $2,620.80 per employee every year. This means businesses with:
- 10 employees lose $26,200 annually;
- 25 employees lose $65,520 annually;
- 50 employees lose $131,040 annually;

- 100 employees lose $262,080 annually;
- 250 employees lose $655,200 annually;
- 500 employees lose $1,310,400 annually;
- 1,000 employees lose $2,626,800 annually...all due to workplace conflict.

These lost dollars could be utilized for expanded benefits, employee development, marketing, or additional personnel. Instead, it's wasted cash, providing no ROA to you, your team or your organization. There's no business model on the planet that would view this as acceptable.

To be effective you must become an expert at leading your organization through the *conflict pigpen*. When conflict is ignored it's disastrous for everyone. On the other hand, effective conflict resolution leads to organizational cultures defined by trust, collaboration and growth. That's a heck of lot better than losing thousands of dollars because of disengaged and stressed employees.

The People Problem

Let's face it, people are difficult. Our personalities are shaped by past experiences, failures, successes and emotional hurts. Collectively they define how we act and react to various situations. They make us optimistic or negative, aggressive or passive, joyful or melancholy, and they always shape the underlying culture. If you're going to build a healthy organization, first you must learn to work with all sorts of difficult personalities.

So, what's they key? One word: *relationships*. Leadership expert John C. Maxwell says, "Relational skills are the most important abilities in leadership." (Maxwell 2005) Successful leaders focus on building meaningful relationships. Period.

Since relationships are foundational to leadership success, and the ability to forge meaningful relationships is a disappearing skillset, the obvious question is, "What are you going to do about it?"

Pigs Everywhere

As a young boy growing up in Mississippi, the importance of character and faith was instilled in me. Attributes such as honesty, love for your neighbor, and hard work were simply a way of life, non-negotiables embedded deep into the fabric of who we were as a family. These foundational truths were taught, however, against a backdrop of intense poverty and difficult circumstances.

My mom, Nita, was energetic, adventurous and excelled in school. A bad decision at the age of fourteen, however, resulted in an unexpected pregnancy. Though she and my father married, at the age of seventeen she was divorced, a 9th grade dropout and the mother of two small boys. But she was a fighter. I watched her work multiple jobs to make ends meet, receive her GED, and then enroll in trade school to make a better life for her family.

As Mom faced life's challenges head-on, she relentlessly forged in us a belief that we aren't defined by yesterday, but by how we shape tomorrow. Circumstances certainly shape and influence us, but they don't define us. I'm thankful to mom for this gift.

Thankfully, mom didn't have to take this journey alone. Her parents, "Dub" and Maggie Thames were by her side all the way. Living next door to my grandparents meant we spent as much time at MamaT's and Papa's as we did at our own house. Because they were so involved in my life it was almost like having two sets of parents providing me with love and encouragement to pursue my dreams. In less than ideal circumstances, they somehow convinced me I could do anything, be anything, or accomplish anything my heart desired. Everything was within my grasp.

Following my parent's divorce, Papa became the primary male figure in my life. I often tell people he taught me how to fish, hunt, chew tobacco, pray…and cuss, not necessarily in that order! He was an amazing man who shaped much of who I am today. Papa also was the consummate "hard worker," working from dawn to sunset only taking short breaks for water or lunch. In his mind a strong work ethic was equally as important as making good grades, something he unapologetically demanded.

Because we lived well below the poverty line, Papa grew most of what we ate. Summers were spent hand-picking corn, peas and beans from his huge garden to put food on the table. He also raised a few chickens, cows and pigs in pens behind the house that provided meat for the freezer. The amount of work required to keep things moving meant all of us had chores, and mine was 'slopping' the hogs. This meant every morning before school I'd go to the hog pen, hold my nose, and feed those dirty animals.

Guess what? I never learned to love pigs. Sure, I enjoyed watching "fake" TV pigs like Miss Piggy, Porky Pig, Piglett and Pumba, but they weren't real. The pigs in the backyard were dirty, aggressive, and smelled horribly. Now, I understand a lot of people own pet pigs. In fact, over 1-million people in the U.S., including celebrities like Madonna, Miley Cyrus, and George Clooney, have traded in their cats, dogs and goldfish for pet porkers. But here's my theory: I don't think they've actually ever 'slopped' a real pig! If they had they would know pigs are filthy and they stink. Most important, if you get too close you end up smelling like them!

Never Wrestle with Pigs

George Benard Shaw evidently slopped a few pigs in his lifetime because he clearly understood the realities of getting entangled with them. Shaw famously said, "I learned a long time ago to never wrestle with a pig. You both get dirty and the pig likes it." He was correct. If you get in the mud with a pig it usually doesn't end well! You come out of the pigpen having wasted your time and needing a bath. The pig just continues to wallow and makes no real change. In both cases, the pig wins!

Sometimes, however, you can't avoid the pigpen. Some issues are so important and some personalities so toxic that you only have one option: wrestle the pig. What do you do when that happens?

That's where this book comes in. Over the next chapters we will explore seven Pig Personalities we must navigate to be effective leaders. These pigs are present in every organization and influence how we handle meetings, execute strategy and manage personnel challenges. The Pig Personalities are:

- The Wild Boar (The Bully)
- The Warthog (The Passive-Aggressive)
- The Pot-bellied Pig (The People Pleaser)
- The Haughty Pig (The Know-It-All)
- The Sow (The Whiner)
- The Piglet (The Want-to-Be Expert)
- Wilbur the Pig (The Ideal Employee)

Your ability to strategically interact with these personalities will directly impact the long-term success of your organization as well as your personal leadership potential. The question isn't *"Will you have to wrestle pigs?"*, but rather *"How will you do it?"*

Let's get started!

Two

THE WILD BOAR

(The Bully)

Now, what do you have to say before I tear you apart?
— Butch, *The Little Rascals*, 1937

G rowing up my favorite after-school activity was watching classic reruns of Hal Roach's *The Little Rascals*. These short black-and-white films, produced from 1922-1944, focus on a group of poor children and their daring adventures. Even today, characters such as Spanky, Alfalfa, Buckwheat, Darla and Porky live on as cultural icons.

The main antagonist in the series was Butch, a stereotypical school-age bully who notoriously gave the gang fits. I've spent many afternoons laughing as Butch rolled up his sleeves, balled his fist and shouted to Alfalfa, "Now, what do you have to say before I tear you apart!" In the real world, however, bullying isn't a laughing matter. It creates stress, causes serious health challenges, and contributes to an unhealthy self-esteem.

So, what does a bully look like? We can learn a lot from Butch because he shares many of the same characteristics of real-life bullies, whether on the playground or in the workplace (Aurora 2017):

- He has to be in control;
- He enjoys dominating those around him;
- He has a short-fuse;
- He enjoys making others afraid;

- He always blames his victim; and,
- He uses his superior strength and size to intimidate others.

It looks like our old friend Butch is the quintessential Wild Boar, and "poor, poor Alfalfa" is the stereotypical victim. Sadly, Alfalfa's in good company. Research shows that Wild Boars (bullies) are a major problem, with nearly half of all U.S. workers being affected by workplace bullying. (Kane 2019)

What is Workplace Bullying?

The Workplace Bullying Institute (WBI) defines workplace bullying as "repeated, health-harming mistreatment of one or more persons (the targets) by one or more perpetrators that takes one or more of the following forms:
- Verbal abuse;
- Offensive conduct/behaviors (including nonverbal) which are threatening, humiliating, or intimidating;
- Work interference - sabotage - which prevents work from getting done." (Workplace Bullying Institute n.d.)

WBI goes on to point out that workplace bullying:
- Is driven by perpetrators' need to control the targeted individual(s);
- Is initiated by bullies who choose their targets, timing, location, and methods;
- Is a set of acts of commission (doing things to others) or omission (withholding resources from others);
- Requires consequences for the targeted individual;
- Escalates to involve others who side with the bully, either voluntarily or through coercion;
- Undermines legitimate business interests when bullies' personal agendas take precedence over work itself; and,

- Is akin to domestic violence at work, where the abuser is on the payroll. (Workplace Bullying Institute n.d.)

The Wild Boar in Action

Wild Boars are easy to spot because they have one goal: to get their way...no matter what. They're driven by their own selfish ambitions and will overpower, runover, minimize and destroy anyone or anything that stands in their path. While they use a wide-range of techniques for their attacks, Wild Boars are notoriously arrogant, abusive, aggressive and intimidating. Trust me, these are not the personalities you want to meet in the pigpen alone.

Although Wild Boars are sometimes coworkers, that's usually not the case. In fact, in seventy-two percent of workplace bullying cases the manager is the guilty party. So, how do you know if you're being bullied? If you can answer "Yes" to the following questions, there's a strong chance you're working for a Wild Boar:

- Are you being verbally abused or minimized?
- Are you being intimidated or threatened?
- Has your commitment to the organization been questioned?
- Have papers on your desk been removed without your knowledge?
- Is someone undermining your work?
- Are you consistently assigned unrealistic deadlines?
- Is important information being withheld from you?
- Are your emails and calls being ignored by your supervisor?
- Are you blamed for mistakes or missed deadlines that weren't your responsibility?
- Have you been blocked from a promotion?

- Are you excluded from important meetings or social events?
- Are meetings you need to attend scheduled when you have a conflict?
- Are important decisions made while you are out of the office?

A Presidential Wild Boar

Lyndon B. Johnson, the 36th President of the United States, was one of the most successful and powerful political leaders in U.S. history. Prior to ascending to the presidency following the Kennedy assassination in 1963, Johnson had served as the 37th Vice-President of the United States (1961-1963), as well as a powerful member of the U.S. Senate (1949-1961) and six terms in the U.S. House of Representatives (1937-1949). Johnson's influence was evident in 1955 when Senate Democrats selected him as Majority Leader at the age of 46, making him the youngest Majority Leader in history.

An imposing figure, Johnson leveraged his 6'4", 200-pound frame to force buy-in to his legislative agenda. Ruthless, ambitious, competitive and forceful, Johnson consolidated all these traits into "The Johnson Treatment," described by recipients as having "a large St. Bernard licking your face and pawing you all over." (Dallek 2005)

"The Treatment" could last anywhere from ten minutes or four hours and it would come whenever and wherever Johnson might find a fellow Senator or politician within his radius. Its tone could be and included supplication, accusation, cajolery, exuberance, scorn, tears, complaint and the hint of threat." All of these elements together brought out the spectrum of human emotions. Its velocity was breathtaking, and it was all in one direction. Interjections from the target were rare and even if they were attempted, Johnson would anticipate them before they could be successfully delivered. He would move in close, with his face a mere millimeter from his target, his eyes widening and narrowing, his eyebrows fluctuating, his pockets stuffed with clippings, memos, statistics and other research he had gathered on his target. All the elements LBJ used, "mimicry, humor, and the genius of analogy," in "The Treatment" rendered the target stunned, helpless, and obedient. (Mark Howard Long 2010-2011)

Figure 1:
President Lyndon B. Johnson gives "The Treatment" to Abe Fortas (Okamoto 1965)

Surviving a Wild Boar Attack

When you're under attack by a Wild Boar there are specific actions you can take to protect yourself. Remember, the goal of the Wild Boar is to get their way, and they try to do this by minimizing you and your ideas. Hold you ground and don't let it happen.

Interrupt the Attack

In elementary school I suffered from a severe stuttering problem making me an easy prey for Wild Boars. My speech impediment, coupled with our family's poverty, negatively impacted my self-esteem and on many days left me gripped with fear.

After withstanding months of aggressive attacks by our resident playground bully, one afternoon I finally reached a breaking point. In the midst of one of his attacks, as he shouted insults and threats, I did something I'd never done before. I closed my eyes and punched him directly in the nose!

I'm not proud of it...but honestly, I don't regret it. From that moment on there was no more teasing, no more slapping me on the head, and no more name calling. The bullying stopped because I stood up and interrupted the attack.

Now, I'm not advocating *actual* physical violence. That will result in termination, counseling or even worse, jail time! If you're being attacked by a Wild Boar, however, I am encouraging that you *figuratively* punch them in the nose. Stand up. Speak up. Get off the ropes. Don't let them continue the attack.

Wild Boars don't know how to respond when they're challenged. I wish I could count the number of times I've seen a Wild Boar in tears after being confronted about his behavior. They thrive on overpowering, but generally don't have the courage to withstand a counter assault. Interrupt the attack!

Call Them by Name

One of the foundational tactics of Wild Boars is to dehumanize their victim. They do this by blocking out all personal and emotional connection. When you're being attacked, simply call the person by name over and over again. Use phrases such as, "John, the tone you're using is not helping," or "I want to find a solution, John, but this approach is unacceptable." Personalizing the attack gives you a definite advantage.

Maintain Eye Contact

Most people avoid eye contact when threatened. Unfortunately, this seldom helps because it signals fear and insecurity. When the Wild Boar attacks dig deep within and stare them in the eyes. Resist the temptation to look down or away. Stare them squarely in the eyes and force them to speak to you, not at you. It makes a huge difference in humanizing the conversation and places you on equal emotional ground.

Control Your Emotions

When you're under attack it's easy to lose control of your emotions. Don't let it happen. As a NCAA sports official, I've always taken this stance: when tempers flare, at least there'll be one person who isn't crazy! When Wild Boars attack, take a deep breath, keep your voice calm and even, and take control of the situation. This means making an intentional decision to defuse the situation rather than responding in a way that escalates negative emotions.

Document Everything

If you're experiencing a Wild Boar attack it's important to keep a written record of all the details. There are situations where the attacks are so intense and relentless that others have to be brought into the loop. Make sure you have all the information you need to make your case. This includes any emails and meeting notes, as well as details from any verbal attacks witnessed by others. While using this information is generally a last resort, prepare for the worst case and document everything.

Although no one likes to confront Wild Boars, ignoring them isn't an option. Left unchecked they intensify their attacks and broaden their target base. When this happens, everyone is a potential target and no hiding place is safe.

Decide today to stand up the Wild Boar. He's killing your culture, destroying relationships, and setting your organization up for long-term failure.

Three

THE WARTHOG

(The Passive-Aggressive)

Although I express myself with some degree of pleasantry the purpose of my words is entirely serious.
— Robert Louis Stevenson, *New Arabian Nights*

I love all things Disney. After all, it really is the most magical place on earth! Over the past thirty years we've visited the Magic Kingdom® over thirty times (don't judge me), often meticulously following a "Disney Commando Plan" to ensure every minute is fully leveraged. We've also spent a small fortune on t-shirts, toys and princess dresses designed to bring smiles and magic to our three daughters. Heck, my middle daughter, Lizzie, even had a Disney-themed wedding reception complete with character artwork, themed food stations and lighting effects based on her favorite Disney movies.

While we love pretty much every Disney movie ever released, one of our all-time favorites is *The Lion King*. Throughout the story there are many wonderful characters including Simba, Nala, Mufasa, Zazu and Timon, but my personal favorite is the gluttonous warthog, Pumbaa. It's hard not to love Pumbaa because of his childlike naivety and innocence. Although his sidekick, Timon, would say otherwise, the warthog is actually the one with the brains:

Timon: ...who's the brains of the outfit?
Pumbaa: Uh...
Timon: My point, exactly.
—*Timon and Pumbaa*

In real life, however, warthogs are not so loveable. When Disney released character photos in advance of their 2019 live-action remake of *The Lion King*, many people were angry that Pumbaa looked like...well...a real, live warthog. As one writer said, "So, okay. I get that in everyone's mind Pumbaa is an adorable red cartoon animal with a big goofy smile and comically thin legs, but here's the thing: This is what warthogs look like." (Hughes 2019)

In the wild, warthogs are dangerous. They hang out in groups, called *sounders*, sharing their surroundings with many animals. While on the surface everything looks calm, don't be fooled. When a warthog is threatened it withdraws to a sunken burrow where it waits to attack its prey hidden from full sight. Though their attacks are not in the open, they can inflict substantial pain and death. So much for nonconfrontational!

What's a Warthog?

We've all seen passive-aggressive behavior before...and perhaps been guilty of it ourselves. Simply defined, passive-aggression is a "deliberate and masked way of expressing hidden anger". (Long, Long, & Whitson, 2009) Warthogs, or passive-aggressive personalities, use a variety of behaviors to get back at others, most often without their colleagues ever becoming aware of their anger. Passive-Aggression is a common method for venting anger in the workplace because it happens "in the burrows" largely hidden from plain sight.

In a sense, it's the perfect workplace crime because it allows employees to intentionally sabotage productivity and undermine others' success – and do it without leaving incriminating evidence. (Chibana n.d.)

The Warthog in Action

Passive-aggressive warthogs are everywhere, and they have one primary goal: to undermine without being obvious. They're sitting in the office next to you, drinking coffee in the breakroom, leading meetings in the C-suite, and unfortunately, far too often they're staring back in the mirror. While all the pig personalities are prevalent, the warthog is the most common and potentially the most destructive personality in your work culture. Not only will this behavior kill a great business, it will obliterate the self-esteem of the people attacked.

Warthogs can't be allowed to remain in hiding. You have to "smoke them out." Leaders must understand how they act, then take action to address the behaviors.

Passive-aggressive Warthogs:
- Don't respond to your emails, continually procrastinate and intentionally miss deadlines;
- Take sarcastic jabs at you in meetings, then respond with "I was only kidding" when confronted;
- On the surface appear to be agreeable and supportive, but behind the scenes will backstab, undercut, and sabotage;
- Constantly tell you to trust their words, but their actions send another message;
- Make promises they have no intention of keeping, often shifting blame when things go wrong;
- Support you to your face, but then disagree or even sabotage things behind your back;

- Shower accolades to you directly, but then take actions to undercut you to coworkers and management;
- Withhold important information to make themselves appear more important while attempting to make others around them fail.

We recently worked with an organization that for a decade was defined by a toxic, passive-aggressive work culture. The place was inundated with Warthogs! Key leaders spent most days looking over their shoulders or pulling "tusks" from their backs, all the time playing a proverbial chess game trying to determine who was on board. They sat in weekly meetings where major decisions were affirmed, only to learn hours later those same decisions were being undermined by the people who hours earlier had indicated their support.

This toxic culture started with several passive-aggressive members of senior leadership, then spread to lower-level employees. As behind-the-scenes alliances were formed, cultural health deteriorated to the point that three CEOS were terminated within eight years, strategically and financially destabilizing the organization. Employee morale plummeted as conversations became defined by negativity and complaining. Competent leaders were forced out and good employees moved on to healthier opportunities. While the behind-the-scenes alliances were strong enough to protect many of the Warthogs responsible for the toxic culture, years of chaos left the organization in shambles and only a shadow of its former success. Even so, all was not lost.

A new CEO was onboarded who understood the underlying culture issues. As a result, he immediately implemented a zero-tolerance policy for insubordination and demanded team loyalty. With new expectations in place, the Warthogs were smoked out and most exited within twelve months. A passive-aggressive culture became defined by teamwork, transparency and organizational health. Now that's a turnaround!

Surviving a Warthog Attack

While it's difficult to smoke-out Warthogs, it's not impossible. Here are some recommendations to get your team focused on positive actions to address passive-aggressive behaviors:

Set Expectations

Reduce the amount of grey area surrounding workloads, deadlines and the quality of what is delivered, by setting clear expectations. This means clearly defining who's responsible and by date.

Specifically Call It Out

When you hear sarcastic comments or observe negative body language, identify it calmly but directly. For example, if someone rolls their eyes, ask "I noticed you rolled your eyes. What caused you to react this way?" When pointing out passive-aggressive behavior, be specific, not general. Point out the problem with facts and details, but do it in a calm, respectful manner.

Encourage Collaboration

Allow people to feel they can openly express their thoughts and opinions, even when they are controversial or not necessarily in line with the rest of the team.

Communicate Face-to-Face

Warthogs often hide behind email. Instead of allowing passive-aggressive personalities to communicate undermine using digital tools, insist on face-to-face communication.

<u>Get Grounded</u>

Be aware of what you're feeling and why. This will help you communicate more openly and effectively and allow you to vent your frustrations in a constructive manner.

<u>Expand Conflict Resolution Skills</u>

Rooting out passive-aggressive will require you to face conflict that head-on. In the end, however, this will be more constructive than letting unresolved issues fester.

Passive-Aggressive Warthogs operate from the bushes, surprising their prey when they least expect it. Make a commitment to call out this dangerous behavior before it spreads throughout your entire team. Failing to do so leaves your entire organization vulnerable to a culture defined by negativity, conflict and low morale.

Four

THE POT-BELLIED PIG

(The People Pleaser)

I cannot give you the formula for success,
but I can give you the formula for failure - which is:
Try to please everybody."
— Herbert Bayard Swope

Have you ever read Aesop's fable, "The Man, the Boy, and the Donkey"?

A man and his son were once going with their Donkey to market. As they were walking along by its side a countryman passed them and said: "You fools, what is a Donkey for but to ride upon?"

So the Man put the Boy on the Donkey and they went on their way. But soon they passed a group of men, one of whom said: "See that lazy youngster, he lets his father walk while he rides."

So the Man ordered his Boy to get off, and got on himself. But they hadn't gone far when they passed two women, one of whom said to the other: "Shame on that lazy lout to let his poor little son trudge along."

Well, the Man didn't know what to do, but at last he took his Boy up before him on the Donkey. By this time they had come to the town, and the passers-by began to jeer and point at them. The Man stopped and asked what they were scoffing at. The men said: "Aren't you ashamed of yourself for overloading that poor Donkey of yours—you and your hulking son?"

The Man and Boy got off and tried to think what to do. They thought and they thought, till at last they cut down a pole, tied the Donkey's feet to it, and raised the pole and the Donkey to their shoulders. They went along amid the laughter of all who met them till they came to Market Bridge, when the Donkey, getting one of his feet loose, kicked out and caused the Boy to drop his end of the pole. In the struggle the Donkey fell over the bridge, and [with] his fore-feet being tied together he was drowned.

"That will teach you," said an old man who had followed them:

PLEASE ALL, AND YOU WILL PLEASE NONE.

(Aesop 1909–14.)

Ok, I admit it. I want people to like me.

The importance of building meaningful relationships was instilled deep within my character from as far back as I can remember. The Golden Rule, "Do unto others as you would have them do unto you," was simply a way of life for my family. It was a non-negotiable, like attending church on Sunday and being respectful to my elders. And it certainly wasn't open for debate.

Not much has changed. I still want people to see me as kind, respectful and servant-minded. I value being empathetic to others and going the extra mile to assist when needed. Sometimes, however, I go too far. In those moments my desire to please others overpowers my own personal and emotional well-being.

It's also one thing to *care* about what others think, but it's much worse when we begin *worrying* about it. When this happens, every decision we make, every presentation we deliver, and every disagreement becomes personal. Dr. Frank Pollard, the long-time pastor at First Baptist Church, Jackson, Mississippi gave great advice regarding this subject. After shared with Dr. Pollard that I was concerned some people weren't happy with a decision I had made. He looked at me and said, "Lavon, it's none of your business what other people think about you." That piece of advice changed how I view other's opinion of me. Do I still care what they think? Of course. Do I worry about it? No. My responsibility is to use the best information available to make the best decision possible. I'm honored to serve others, but it's not my job to please them.

The key is to find balance.

What's a Pot-Bellied Pig?

Everyone loves a Pot-bellied pig because they have one goal: to make everyone happy. People-pleasers are sociable, lovable and agreeable, but can easily:

- Wear themselves out trying to please everyone;
- Take on tasks they could easily assign;
- Avoid taking charge and have difficulty making decisions;
- Sugarcoat responses and resist honest feedback;
- Portray a false image of friendliness;
- Overlook their own plans, feelings, and needs;
- Tolerate bad performance or behavior;
- Become resentful when things don't play out in their favor;
- Because they overcommit then can end up resentful and unreliable;
- Manipulate people to avoid asking for what they want; and,
- Because of overload they eventually meltdown.

The Pot-Bellied Pig in Action

My friend, Carol, was the definitive people-pleaser. She was always the first one to volunteer for tasks no one else wanted to do. If her team got behind on a project, Carol was the first to jump in to save the day. Even worse, when other team members failed to honor their commitments or meet their deadlines, she always said, "that's OK," then stayed late to fill in the gap.

As you can imagine, everyone loved Carol! What was there not to like? She was kind, compassionate and her co-workers appreciated her willingness to help them out. Being liked, however, isn't the same as being respected. Often her requests would go unanswered or were delayed. After all, with other pressing issues on the agenda she would certainly understand. And while she had management responsibilities, her team was undisciplined due to her unwillingness to confront problems. She worked longer hours than everyone else because she was involved in everyone's projects. Even worse, others on her team had been promoted although she was carrying the majority of the workload.

Eventually, the weight of people-pleasing took its toll. Overworked, stressed-out and underpaid, Carol resigned from her "dream job," effectively throwing a grenade into her career path.

If this sounds familiar, you're probably a Pot-Bellied Pig! Ask yourself the following questions to help clarify if you've slipped into a people-pleasing mentality:

- Do you let others run over you?
- Do you do things out of obligation, and then feel resentful?
- Do you avoid conflict like the plague?
- Do you have a hard time saying "no?"
- Do you constantly worry about disappointing others?
- Do you bend over backwards for other people, often to your own detriment?
- Do you fear people will not view you as "nice" if you don't accommodate them?

If you find yourself answering yes to these questions, then it's time to make some changes in how you relate to those around you.

Although pleasing others at your own expense might gain you short-term approval, the long-term effects can be catastrophic.

Surviving a Pot-Bellied Pig ~~Attack~~ Lovefest

If you work with a people-pleaser, or have those tendencies yourself, there are things you can do to get out of the pigpen.

Build Trust – Because people-pleasers crave acceptance, it's important the relationships be grounded in trust. When this happens, it is no longer a transactional relationship, but one based on valuing the individual as a person.

Encourage – Ironically, the Pot-Bellied Pig's weakness is based on a desire to do something good. They aren't mean-spirited and aggressive, nor is their goal to undermine other team members. Because of this, they must understand that, while their intentions are honorable, the results create an environment where they cannot succeed.

Be Specific – Speaking in generalities will not work with people-pleasers. Saying, "I think you should stop volunteering to take other people's responsibilities" will be met with a simple, "Yes, I agree." The problem is, nothing will change. Instead, be specific with your concerns: "Renee, volunteering to make copies for Larry is very thoughtful, but it resulted in you missing an important deadline. Moving forward, check with me before taking on additional projects." Pot-bellied Pigs need to hear exactly what created the problem and how to address it.

Coach boundaries – When coaching people-pleasers, the most important tool at our disposal is the concept of personal and professional boundaries. For example, a desire to help others is admirable, but repeatedly working overtime is unhealthy. Although it takes time and energy, assisting Pot-Bellied Pigs with strategies to define healthy boundaries not only improves their life, but promotes overall organizational health.

The Pot-Bellied Pig is the most lovable, agreeable and cooperative of all the pig personalities. Their focus on gaining acceptance from others comes from a good place, but the results often cause damage to their own relationships, emotional health, and long-term career objectives. Use honest and transparent encouragement to help people-pleasers understand how their actions are actually hurting themselves and the organization. Then coach boundaries to help them develop a strategy for success.

Five

THE HAUGHTY PIG

(The Know-It-All)

It is better to keep your mouth closed and let people think you are a fool than to open it and remove all doubt.

— Mark Twain

What do Alexander the Great, Henry VIII, Rush Limbaugh, Tony Soprano and Steven Colbert all have in common? They are all Haughty Pigs, or what is more commonly known as "Insufferable Know-It-Alls." Haughty Pigs have never met a problem they didn't know how to solve. They literally have an answer for everything. These are the folks who strut while sitting down. Although they come in various shapes, sizes and roles, they share a common trait: an unfortunate ability to get on your last nerve!

Over the years I've worked with a lot of Haughty Pigs, but the classic example was "Brad." As president and COO of a $750 million-dollar business, Brad had achieved undeniable success. His years of experience, coupled with his deep industry knowledge, uniquely positioned him for continued professional and financial success. For all practical purposes the sky was his limit, but there was a major problem: he was the definitive Haughty Pig. When facing a challenge there was no need to involve or seek advice from others because Brad knew it all.

On the surface this model seemed to work for several years. Rapid financial growth and carefully controlled optics created an impression that all was well. It wasn't. Within the organization emerging leaders were muzzled, suppressed or simply forced out. Platforms for honest and transparent input were minimized as Brad intentionally seized all major decision-making. Key leaders were relegated to "do as I say" foot soldiers and employees were used as a means to an end. While words like "team" and "collaboration" were commonly used, it all was a smokescreen. As a result, morale declined, shared vision evaporated, and trust was trampled into the ground.

Brad's "know it all" attitude led to a quite predictable outcome. After leaving the organization financially and legally exposed as a result of one of his solo decisions, Brad was unceremoniously dumped by the Board of Directors. Contrary to what he believed, he didn't have all the answers and he certainly wasn't invincible. His Haughty Pig tendencies left him exposed, vulnerable and sadly, unemployed.

What's a Haughty Pig?
You probably don't have to think very hard to identify a "know it all" Haughty Pig. In addition to often being argumentative, condescending and egomaniacs, Haughty Pigs usually have one primary goal: to get their ideas implemented...because they know best. Using their self-ascribed superiority, they are one of the most annoying workplace personalities with a penchant for condescension, showing disrespect for superiors and continually engaging in unnecessary debates with coworkers. Because they present themselves as experts on all topics, Haughty Pigs often monopolize meetings, offer unsolicited advice and dominate even the most basic conversations.

As a general rule, Haughty Pigs bring high levels of professional experience and knowledge to the table. Unfortunately, they know it. As a result, they are notorious for ignoring the opinions of others because their own opinion is always better. While this extreme self-confidence can be intimidating, don't be fooled. Haughty Pigs often struggle with low self-esteem and use their "know it all" personalities to deflect their own anxiety and feelings of inadequacy.

The Haughty Pig in Action

With an attitude of extreme arrogance, Haughty Pigs often torpedo attempts to establish collaborative workplace cultures and healthy teams. In addition, they are characterized by:

High Levels of Aggression

Because Haughty Pigs hold their own opinions in such lofty esteem, they frequently display highly aggressive attitudes towards other members of the team. I recall sitting in a meeting with a senior leadership team that was struggling to develop a culture of transparency and openness. After several meetings, one of the team members mustered enough courage to offer a creative suggestion to a complicated problem. Almost reactively, the team leader responded, "Well, that's the stupidest idea I've ever heard!" As you can imagine, the air immediately left the room, and with it any chance for positive collaboration was squelched. Haughty Pigs consistently exhibit aggressive comments, closed body language and negative facial expressions designed to minimize the contributions of others.

Monopolize Meetings

"Know It All" Haughty Pigs monopolize meetings. Regardless of the issue on the table…they speak. They have opinions about every topic, solutions for every problem and a better option for every strategy. This incessant verbal rambling gets old very quickly and is virtually impossible to stop without a direct confrontation.

Failure? Not My Fault

When something goes wrong or fails to rise to expectations, Haughty Pigs often respond by saying, "It wasn't my idea" or "I wasn't involved in that decision." They relish the role of Monday Morning Quarterback, often second-guessing every decision.

Paint inaccurate pictures

Haughty Pigs almost never give an accurate description of the realities on the ground. When asked, "How are things going," they respond: "Things are amazing! I'm making more money than ever, my clients never question my recommendations, my spouse thinks I'm amazing and we're headed to Europe for a month-long vacation." The reality is usually quite different: they are about to file bankruptcy, their clients have lost confidence in their abilities to produce, their spouse is about to file for divorce, and the closest they'll get to Europe is reading the latest edition of the AAA travel magazine!

Haughty Pigs = Narcissism

While many leaders struggle with narcissistic tendencies, Haughty Pigs embrace them. The secret is to identify the negative traits and take steps to remove them from your leadership style. As a former professor once reminded me, "To be forewarned is to be forearmed!" This being true, it is imperative leaders identify these tendencies and take steps to protect themselves from narcissistic behavior.

The *Diagnostic and Statistical Manual of Mental Disorders* (DSM-5), published by the American Psychiatric Association, identifies the following personality traits associated with narcissism:

- Having an exaggerated sense of self-importance

- Expecting to be recognized as superior even without achievements that warrant it
- Lying about your achievements and talents
- Being preoccupied with fantasies about success, power, brilliance, beauty or the perfect mate
- Requiring constant admiration
- Having a sense of entitlement
- Expecting special favors and unquestioning compliance with your expectations
- Taking advantage of others to get what you want
- Having an inability or unwillingness to recognize the needs and feelings of others
- Being envious of others and believing others envy you
- Behaving in an arrogant or haughty manner (Mayo Clinic 2017)

Do you have any of these traits? Though difficult to hear, sometimes we're the Haughty Pig! If these traits hit a little too close to home, an immediate attitude adjustment is in order.

Haughty Pigs hurt teams, hurt the organization and most importantly kills your culture. Take immediate steps to identify the culprit and address the behavior, even if it means looking in a mirror and facing a hard reality.

Surviving a Haughty Pig Attack

Dealing with Haughty Pigs can be extremely frustrating because of their arrogance and aggressiveness. Even so, there are some basic tools we can use to mitigate the encounter.

First, recognize them as an expert. As already mentioned, Haughty Pigs are often extremely knowledgeable and benefit from years of professional experience. Because of this we need their input and expertise. They bring invaluable resources to the table and their insight must be leveraged.

The second step, which is critical, is to point them to new ideas. This can be accomplished be stating, "That is an amazing idea and I think it will work. Obviously, your experience in this area is invaluable to our team. What if we also considered …?"

Third, enlist their help. Inviting them to participate in strategy sessions, lead projects and provide ongoing feedback keeps them at the table, allows the entire team to benefit from their expertise, and creates additional opportunities for coaching.

Fourth, Haughty Pigs must receive consistent and direct feedback. If you supervise a Haughty Pig, this is a non-negotiable. Often their "know it all" attitudes are wrecking their career goals and potential for long-term success. In your role as supervisor, you are responsible to coach them on the negative impact their behaviors are having on their career objectives. When giving feedback always focus on specific actions that have created problems for them or the team, never generalities that can't be specifically identified.

Other times we look up and find Haughty Pigs seated across the table from us in the form of a colleague. This can get a little tricky. Should you address it or simply ignore it and move on? This decision always has to be grounded in the status of the relationship. Start by asking permission: "Can I talk to you about something?" This sets the stage for a positive conversation. You can then talk about your direct observations, putting an emphasis on your colleague's expertise and the consequences of flaunting it: "We all know you are an expert in this area, but when you gave the answer right away, everyone else immediately shut down. Did you notice that?"

The worse-case scenario is when the Haughty Pig is your boss! If this is the case, there are two important ground-rules that can help you successfully survive the attack. First, ask yourself "Is this battle worth fighting?" If not, leave it alone. There are some battles that simply aren't worth it. Remember, if you fight every battle, you'll be too tired to fight the ones that really matter! Second, if you determine it has to be addressed then focus on highlighting their expertise while simultaneously encouraging them to consider other ideas. Ask questions that lead with "Have you ever…" or "What if…" to promote a sense of openness. Also, arm yourself with relevant data to support an alternative position rather than relying on good ideas.

Regardless of where the Haughty Pigs sits in your org chart, NEVER place yourself in compete mode. Argumentative debates or direct competition will never change the behavior of a Haughty Pig. In the end, you end up looking like a Haughty Pig yourself. Finally, when dealing with "know it alls" use the Reagan Doctrine: give them the credit! President Ronald Reagan kept a plaque on his desk in the Oval Office that read, "There is no limit to what a man can do or where he can go if he does not mind who gets the credit." That's a great philosophy for dealing with virtually everyone in your life, but it's extremely effective in neutralizing the infamous Haughty Pig.

Six

THE SOW

(The Whiner)

Never tell your problems to anyone...
20% don't care and the other 80% are glad you have them.
— Lou Holtz

In October 1347, twelve ships docked at the Sicilian port of Messina having arrived from the Black Sea. People gathered on the docks were horrified to realize that most sailors aboard the ships were dead, and those still alive were gravely ill and covered in black boils that oozed blood and pus. Although officials ordered the "death ships" to immediately exit the harbor, it was too late. The Bubonic Plaque had been introduced to Europe and the results would be disastrous. Over the next five years, the "Black Death" would kill more than 20 million people in Europe – almost one-third of the continent's population. (History.com 2019)

Interestingly, many businesses and organizations are facing a cultural plague raging through their halls, cubicles and C-suite offices. Though not literally taking lives, it is nonetheless decimating workplace environments while leaving employee morale in shambles. It's the plague of *chronic complaining* and it's being spread by a dangerous pig personality, The Sow.

What's a Sow?

The Sow is gender neutral and prevalent in most organizations. These people complain and whine about everything:

The temperature is too hot…or it's too cold.
The workload is too heavy…or they're bored.
The meeting is too long…or we didn't cover everything.
The leader is too cocky…or he's too meek.
The boss is too young…or she's too old.

It really doesn't matter what the issue is, the goal of the Sow is simply to whine and for someone…anyone…to listen.

Another important trait of the Sow, or whiner, is they see problems worse than they really are. The most basic request, or the slightest problem is always exaggerated to a worse-case scenario:

A simple accounting error is going to lead to financial ruin.
A rude comment is communicated as a full-frontal attack.
A request to make 5 copies is presented as a 500-page report.
A mistake by a coworker is shared with everyone in the office.
A client's question is presented as intense customer dissatisfaction.

And offering solutions doesn't help. In fact, it only makes the Sow whine more.

The most dangerous trait, however, is the fact misery loves company. Sows are negative and pessimistic, and they want everyone around them to feel the same way. In fact, they'll pull everyone and anyone into the pigpen with them, spreading the negativity plaque throughout the entire office culture.

The Sow in Action

I haven't worked with a lot of Sows, primarily because it's a personality I intentionally avoid. We've seen the damage they do to cultures so, when spot them we take quick action to get them out. No apologies here. The Sow isn't welcome.

With that said, Jess slipped through the filter. Pleasant and winsome when we hired her, it took a couple years to realize she was almost single-handedly driving negativity beneath the surface. Though she initially operated under the radar, her true nature eventually surfaced, and as she became more comfortable her negativity became more aggressive. Jess complained about everything and everybody. No one was left unscathed.

One of Jess' greatest "gifts" was an ability to offer critiques on projects...after the fact. Truth is, many of her post-mortem takedowns contained good observations. Unfortunately, she never offered valid input up front. Her primary strength was to tear down and criticize on the backend of a project.

After numerous attempts at coaching and setting expectations, Jess was eventually terminated. Now for the big surprise: morale immediately stabilized and the overall culture realigned overnight. The carrier of the plague had been neutralized. The only regret was we didn't do it two years sooner!

Surviving a Sow Attack

Dealing with Sows is exhausting, depressing and has a direct impact on your emotional, mental and physical well-being. As a result, when this pig personality is identified we recommend acting immediately, decisively and with clear boundaries.

The most important step is to call out the behavior. Too many times coworkers and supervisors ignore the whining hoping it will simply go away. It won't. Left unaddressed the negativity will intensify and spread, eventually overtaking your entire organizational culture. For leaders who don't mind conflict, dealing with the Ole' Sow is easy. For others, just the anticipation of calling out this type of confrontation causes stress and anxiety. If this is you, try saying something like, "I know you're unhappy about this, but this level of negativity is unacceptable." Clearly define how you expect the Sow to behave moving forward, as well as the consequences for ongoing negativity. Sometimes just confronting the issue will help get the Sow personality under control.

Unfortunately, other times it doesn't. Ryan was the definitive Sow personality. A partner in a major accounting firm, Ryan was a constant whiner and didn't mind spewing negativity to anyone within earshot. After sitting through several minutes of complaining about the long hours during tax season, I used a technique called bridging to refocus the conversation. "Ryan," I said, "I'm sorry you guys have to work like this during the height of tax season, but the good thing is things will let up after April 15. You'll have lots of time with family, where are you guys planning to go on vacation this summer when things slow down?" Bridging is designed to pivot the conversation to a new topic and get the whiner onto something more positive. If you intentionally use this technique, you'll be surprised how many times you can shape the tone and focus of the conversation.

One final recommendation: the best advice is to avoid contact with the Sow whenever possible. As already mentioned, complaining is extremely contagious and the best way to avoid "catching" the negativity is to go the other direction.

No casual conversations.
No lunch meetings.
No coffee breaks.
Absolutely nothing.

Put on a symbolic surgical mask and protect yourself. These are the people that prompted someone to say, "Stay away from negative people. They have a problem for every solution." That's great advice for dealing with the whiners and complainers!

The Sow will devastate your organizational culture. Once the personality has been identified, call it out, set the boundaries, then place them on an immediate 90-day plan of correction. If they don't correct, remove them from the organization as soon as possible.

Trust me, it won't get better.

Seven

THE PIGLET

(The Great Pretender)

I am the wisest man alive, for I know one thing, and that is that I know nothing."

— Socrates

Dr. Gordon McHenry played a pivotal role in my life. A life-long physician, "Dr. Mac" was from the old school. On more than one occasion he knocked on our door late at night, wearing slippers with medical bag in hand, to take care of our daughters when they were sick. No bill ever came. Just a hug, a smile, and a quiet confidence that comes when the doctor says everything's ok. That was Dr. Mac.

But he was more than a physician, he was a friend who invested in our family in countless way. In 1993 cash was not a common thing around our house. As a "starving seminary student" the rare extra income went to buy shoes for my girls, repair aging vehicles, or take care of any one of the unexpected expenses that come your way when you're just getting started. There was certainly no room for a Broadway show. That's where Dr. Mac and his wife, Mrs. Millie, stepped in.

On this day Dr. Mac called and said, "Lavon, have you and Wendy seen *Phantom of the Opera*?" I vividly remember thinking, "No, and I have no interest in going to the opera!" Fortunately, in a rare occasion for that chapter of my life, my brain muzzled my mouth and I simply responded, "No sir." Dr. Mac then said, "Millie and I want to give you and Wendy tickets to see *Phantom* in

New Orleans." Honestly, I wasn't very excited. As a fulltime student trying to balance school, family and work, the last thing I wanted to do was drive 2 hours to hear overweight singers belt out 3 hours of lyrics in a language I didn't understand. Obviously, I was ignorant to the fact that the musical was in English. After a brief pause, I somewhat begrudgingly replied, "That would be awesome." Worst case was a chance to take Wendy on a fancy date…and I didn't have to pay for it.

On the appointed night we settled into our seats at the historic Saenger Theater in the Crescent City fully expecting to make an early exit. When the orchestra sounded the first note of the overture, however, my life changed forever. Thanks to Dr. Mac and Mrs. Mille, that night launched a life-long love for the arts. Since then we've attended more Broadway shows than I can count. New York. London. Nashville. Dallas. Houston. Atlanta.

Broadway musicals use music, sets, and engaging storylines to mesmerize you for 2½ hours. Equipped with these tools of the trade, skilled actors magically transport you into a *pretend* world that allows you to escape the realities of everyday life. For a time, their created world appears to be real.

Following a performance of *Phantom* in Dallas several years ago (we've seen it eleven times), Wendy and I were fortunate to meet the lead. I'll admit it was a bit disconcerting. Moments earlier he had drawn me into his world of romance, conflict and heartbreak. Now he stood before me as…well…a normal man. I felt betrayed. He wasn't the Phantom at all. The character he had created was not real. He was *pretending*.

Organizations are filled with pretenders as well. They present themselves as experts, but they aren't experts at all. Sometimes they lack knowledge, other times they lack experience. In both cases they lack the skills to get the job done. Some call them actors or frauds. For us, they are the quintessential Piglet, the Great Pretender.

What's the Piglet?

Piglets, or the Great Pretenders, are those in your business or organization who have lots of ideas, but lack experience or professional growth to have credibility. They crave respect and admiration from others and present themselves as experts. The problem is they aren't experts at all. Although their goal is to have a seat at the table, they aren't ready.

They *really* are pretending.

The Piglet in Action

Organizations often assume Piglets are young and lack experience, and sometimes that's correct. Millennials, born between 1981 and 1996, are the largest segment in the workplace and have vastly changed the workplace landscape. With that said, according to CNBC the American workplace is about to be radically changed forever.

> *A new generation is starting to enter the workforce, and the office as you know it could be about to change dramatically. Generation Z — people born after 1996 — is about to hit the working world in a big way....Gen Z accounts for 61 million people in the U.S., a number that's already larger than Generation X and two-thirds the size of the baby boomers.* (Morris 2018)

Because of their dependence on technology, Gen Z struggles with basic communication skills and require intentional training on skills that boomer and millennials excelled in such as handling calls and writing emails. In addition, because they were raised with less emphasis on face-to-face communications, they are unprepared for areas such as customer service and conflict resolution. This skills gap will require intentional training strategies in areas long considered foundational. In the emerging work culture, soft skill training will need to reign supreme.

It's important to understand that younger workers are not the only Piglets out there. An employee who has been with a company for twenty years but refused to grow and develop fits this category as well. Just as youthfulness isn't an absolute indicator of incompetence, age doesn't guarantee competence. It's more about professional growth, a desire to learn, and flexibility that defines a successful employee.

I recently challenged one of my clients to be open to a new idea being presented by leadership. "This will never work," he responded. When I asked how he knew that, he said, "I know what I'm talking about. I have thirty years of experience in this industry." Because he notoriously changes jobs every two years, I reminded him he only had two years of experience that he had repeated fifteen times. He actually was using the exact same methods, approaches and strategies from thirty years ago. He was an older Piglet, but a Piglet still.

How to Survive a Piglet Attack

With lack of experience and marginal soft skills on one end of the spectrum, and a failure to aggressively embrace professional development and growth on the other, how do leaders navigate a modern work culture filled with Piglets?

Be Open to Their Ideas

As leaders our natural tendency is to ignore or minimize ideas that lack experience to back them up. In the emerging workplace culture this will be extremely risky. Successful leaders will embrace the creativity and energy of an expanding younger workforce and create an environment that promotes collaborative problem-solving, creativity and outside-the-box management practices. Most importantly, actively listen to their ideas. You may be surprised at what they bring to the table.

Focus on Mentoring

Mentoring and professional coaching is a critical tool in dealing with Piglets in the workplace, both those who lack experience as well as those who have failed to grow professionally. Intentional relationships are a foundational element for developing successful strategies for improving Piglet skill sets. This targeted skill enhancement is best accomplished through one-on-one mentoring relationships and will produce the quickest improvement in deficient areas.

Establish Clear Expectations

We all need to know our job expectations. If an area is lacking, then the responsibility falls to the leader to clearly articulate the challenge and assist in providing a strategy for improvement. When it comes to what's expected, there should be no grey area. Lay out the expectations then hold the Piglet accountable for making consistent progress towards improvement.

Provide Honest Feedback

The "everyone gets a trophy" mentality has detrimentally impacted a large segment of the younger workforce. This is only made worse when supervisors fail to give open and honest feedback regarding quality of work issues. If it's not great, don't say it is! A better approach is to highlight what is good, then offer constructive feedback on what can be improved. This is imperative when it comes to Piglets lacking experience.

Likewise, Piglets who need to develop flexibility and creativity shouldn't be given a pass simply because they've been with the organization for a long time. If employees have lost a step because of a failure to embrace change or stagnated skill sets, transparent coaching must be a priority.

As Gen Z hits the workforce, organizations must embrace intentional professional strategies focusing on soft skills such as communication, conflict resolution and customer service. While these were considered basic skills with previous generations, this is no longer the case. They will have to be intentionally developed moving forward.

Experienced Piglets will be required to continually expand their creative thinking, technological proficiency and collaborative problem-solving skills. Leaders that are flexible and can embrace non-traditional approaches to management and teambuilding will be in high demand. To succeed, experienced Piglets will need to embrace these qualities.

Organizations who refuse to get in front of these skill deficits will find themselves surrounded by Piglets of all sizes, shapes and ages. The key is to aggressively train and mentor the Piglet to position them for ongoing success.

Eight

WILBUR THE PIG

(The Ideal Employee)

Perfection is not attainable, but if we chase perfection, we can catch excellence.
— Vince Lombardi

As I began my quest to identify the perfect pig, it became obvious I was facing a fairly monumental task. Thankfully, I had two things working in my favor. First, having raised three daughters I've spent many hours watching animated movies. Second, I was blessed with an amazing high school literature teacher, Sarah Jones, who inspired in me a love for reading. With these in my pigpen arsenal I immediately knew the perfect pig personality: Wilbur.

Written by E.B. White and published in 1952, *Charlotte's Web* is a classic of children's literature that tells the story of a pig named Wilbur and his growing friendship with a spider named Charlotte. When Wilbur is in danger of being butchered by the farmer, Charlotte writes messages praising Wilbur in her web in order to persuade the farmer to let him live.

As part of the "research phase" of the project I re-watched the movie...several times. This heartwarming story highlights the unique personality of Wilbur as he navigates relationships, change, growth and ultimately loss. And yes, I cried, but don't judge me. If you take the time to watch it, you'll cry too.

What's a Wilbur?

Wilbur is the ideal employee. His primary goal is to make a difference in the lives of those around him, as well as the organization he serves. He's not autocratic, aggressive or passive, but instead embodies respect, collaboration and efficiency.

Wilbur in Action

What characteristics define Wilber, the ideal employee? There are several that are very important.

Has a Grasp on Reality

Although Wilbur is a "happy go lucky" sort of pig, he comes to a very clear understanding of the realities on the ground. Unless something changes, he's heading from the barnyard to the farmer's table. With clarity comes focus!

When we're absorbed in the day-to-day activities of the barnyard, compiling reports, pursuing deadlines, and managing customer relations, it's virtually impossible to work on things that matter. You can't work *on* your business while working *in* your business. Ideal employees have the ability to step back and take the 30,000-foot view. From here things become much clearer: vision, strategy, personnel, problem-solving. When employees get a grasp on the realities facing the organization, individual priorities, silos and kingdoms become secondary to larger needs.

Continually Developing

In the opening pages of *Charlotte's Web*, Wilbur is an emotional and rambunctious pig. The runt of the litter, he is insecure and often feels threatened or bullied by the other animals. As the story develops, however, Wilbur undergoes an amazing transformation. With Charlotte as his mentor, Wilbur embraces a journey of emotional growth. Not only does he become better at relationships, his basic skills also improve in the process. After Charlotte's death, he even assumes responsibility for raising some of her children. That's a lot of growth from the undisciplined pig in the opening pages of the story.

We can learn a lot from Wilbur and his continual development. When confronted with his weaknesses, he intentionally makes efforts to improve. He takes coaching and constructive criticism, and though not always successful, he learns from his mistakes. Even surrounded by difficult barnyard personalities, Wilbur learns how to build meaningful relationships that move his goals forward.

Embraces change

One of the major themes of *Charlotte's Web* focuses on change. As the story develops, we see a consistent changing of the seasons. Wilbur also experiences major changes when his living quarters are transitioned from the farmhouse to the barnyard. In that moment he's no longer a loved house pet, but rather a common farm animal. As he and Fern grow up, they are forced to deal with topics such as death, changing roles and new stages of life. That's some pretty heavy stuff for a children's book don't you think?

How well do you embrace change? Are you resistant or do you lead the charge when change comes your way? Ideal employees understand that change is inevitable, and that often the only thing we can control is our response to it. Embrace change and you will be on your way to becoming an ideal employee.

Understands Limitations

Faced with Wilbur's certain death, Charlotte developed a strategy to raise Wilbur's value and save his life. Each night words were written in her web describing Wilbur's character. Words like:

"Some Pig"
"Radiant"
"Terrific"
"Humble"

As the plan develops, the barn, and Wilbur, become overnight sensations and his life is spared. After all, there's no way Farmer Zukerman could kill a famous pig!

Here's what's interesting. For the plan to be successful, someone had to actually write the words in the web…and Wilbur couldn't write. He instead relied on Charlotte to spin the life-changing messages. Wisely, Wilbur understood his own limitations.

No one can be good at everything. When we realize this and learn to value other skillsets at the table, our organizations can aggressively break through the ceilings we are hitting.

How to Get a Pigpen Full of Wilburs

We all need more Wilburs in our lives, but how do we create an atmosphere where they thrive?

Celebrate Wins – Too many times we run from one project to the next, never taking time to enjoy the success we just experienced. Take time to celebrate when things go well.

Focus on Relationships – Create consistent opportunities for your teams to build meaningful relationships. Attend a ballgame together. Plan a company picnic. Plan a teambuilding retreat. Whatever your approach, make sure people are connecting on a personal level and that relationships are foundational to your organizational DNA.

Make Communication a Priority – No one likes to be in the dark when it comes to critical information. When important decisions are made get that information out to the organization as quickly as possible. When changes are coming never let your teams be blindsided.

Collaborative Problem-Solving – When people feel valued, they become more heavily vested in your organization. One of the best ways to accomplish this is by including them in the problem-solving process. With more people focused on possible solutions, creative approaches and strategies always come to the forefront. While my strategy may be good, other contributions may make it great. Why take a chance on missing that opportunity by not allowing others to contribute to the process?

Make It Personal – In a culture defined by email and text messages, the power of handwritten communication rises to a new level. Take the time to write thank you notes, birthday cards, and congratulatory letters to your team. It shows you value them as individuals, and it places your leadership style in its own class.

If you have to have pigs in your organization, make sure it's the right one! Wilbur, the ideal employee, will bring success, trust and deep relationships that will allow your team to soar above the others. Create a culture where the Wilburs thrive! You'll be glad you did.

Nine

What Kind of Pig are You?
(The Pig Test)

How few there are who have courage enough to own their faults or resolution enough to mend them.
— Benjamin Franklin

As you read this book, it's easy to identify various people who align with one or more of the seven pig personalities. It's natural to think, "Jerry's definitely a Wart Hog" or "Sherry has a lot of Pot-Bellied Pig traits." While all of us can compile a list of primary offenders, we need to be reminded of an important truth: you are somebody's pig! Though difficult to hear, the harsh reality is your personality most likely creates problems for someone on your team.

While none of us wake up, look in the mirror and say, "Today I'm going to be a pig," if we're honest we must admit that on any given day, at any given time, we can become any one of the seven pig personalities. As much as I hate to admit it, I've taken on the personality of all the pigs at one time or another. *Every single one.*

Several years ago, I made the decision to expand our team by hiring younger employees to work as associates in our organization. As a seasoned leader, educator and strategic thinker, I understood the importance of diversifying our leadership structure and tapping into the creativity and energy of Millennials entering the workforce. Although my intentions were honorable, I was unprepared for what followed.

After going through an extensive and exhaustive interview process, we identified and onboarded three highly talented people to join our team. I actually handpicked all three. Almost immediately, however, we realized there were major differences in philosophy related to work schedules, relationships and the ability to weigh-in on major decisions.

I addressed problems as they arose, attempting to listen to their concerns while reminding them of the organizational DNA in which they were working. After clearly outlining the expectations and boundaries for moving forward, I was completely blindsided when our CFO informed me the employees had complained of being bullied. My initial reaction was, "This is ridiculous!" There was zero doubt in my mind that I'd bullied no one. There had been no thrown chairs or screamed profanities. No one had been minimized or embarrassed in front of our team. Accuse me of being firm or demanding, but not a Wild Boar!

Fast forward six months: all three employees were terminated. Truth is, we had no choice. Trust had been damaged beyond repair and relationships had been fractured beyond restoration. Even so, I was left with a sinking feeling that I could have done more.

In the months that followed I conducted an aggressive gut-check in relation to my leadership style and its impact on this situation. As a result, I came to three conclusions:

Was their firing justified? *Yes.*

Could it have been avoided? *Maybe.*

Had I been a Wild Boar? *Probably.*

While I hadn't committed any of the most common stereotypical bullying offences, there were many things I *should* have done differently:

I should have lowered my tone of voice.

I should have listened more intentionally.
I should have coached more specifically.
I should have invested in building deeper relationships.
I should have developed thicker skin.
I should have been more forgiving of mistakes.
I should have avoided negative conversations about my employees.

I realized I had not only been a Wild Boar bully, it was worse. I had experienced a monstrous metamorphosis resulting in a cross between a Wild Boar and a Warthog. A dangerous cross-breed pig, simultaneously a bully and passive-aggressive.

This experience is a reminder of our vulnerability as leaders. Under the cloak of visionary leadership, team building and strategic intentions, we can fail in the area of building effective relationships. Just as important, although we may aspire to be Wilburs, that ever-allusive ideal employee, we can turn into any of the negative pigs in the blink of an eye.

We are offended by someone…
We want to be in control…
We feel threatened…
We want people to like us…
We pretend we have the answers…
We undermine someone behind the scenes…

BAM! Just like that we find ourselves in the pigpen…and we're the pig! But don't despair, we can help! Our team has developed a tool that will give you a better understanding of your individual pig tendencies. Take the test and learn from it. You'll be a stronger leader or employee because of it!

You can find The Pig Test at:
www.CreativeBread.studio/TakeTheTest

Ten

Surviving the Pigpen

(It's All About Relationships)

You can have everything in life you want
if you will just help enough other people get what they want.
— Zig Ziglar

When surrounded by pigs we're left with one final question: how do you survive the pigpen? Beyond all the strategies, recommendations and warnings, it comes down to a single foundational truth: in the end it's all about relationships.

The legendary Zig Ziglar reminded us, "You can have everything in life you want if you will just help enough other people get what they want." Although deceivingly simple, the inherent truth remains: your success or failure as a leader will be determined primarily by one thing…your ability to build meaningful relationships.

Sometimes we'll find ourselves in the pigpen ready to fight all sorts of piggish personalities. Other times we'll look up and realize *we're* the pig and our actions, though possibly unintentionally, have driven our teams to the corner of the pigpen to defend themselves. In these moments of clarity, we must step back, take a breath, and focus on the person staring back at us. In these moments we're reminded it's the relationship that shapes our ability to succeed.
In the middle of wrestling match, it's easy to focus on issues rather than people. If this happens, we will fail. Every single time. We may win individual battles, but at what cost? Great leadership is

built on trust and influence. Those are beyond our reach when we focus on our individual agendas.

I know what you're thinking: "That's all well and good but I don't believe relationships *really* make that big of a difference." Here's a real-life example of how a simple investment in someone else can make all the difference in the world.

When I was seven-years-old my mom, Melissa Russum, insisted I take piano lessons. A musician herself, mom wanted me to experience the joy that music had brought to her life. A side note: this ability to play piano has infused immeasurable beauty into my life and I will be forever grateful to my mom for this amazing gift. But I digress...

Near the end of my first year of lessons, my piano teacher, H.B. Miller, insisted I participate in a keyboard festival being held at a local college. I still remember the little piece I played, a musical masterpiece entitled, "Comanche," that included three chords and a simple, Native American melody. On the day of the event, which took place in June 1974, I played my piece, promptly receiving a certificate from the judges who awarded me an "Excellent" for the virtuoso performance.

I've never really had fans, but my grandmother, Maggie Thames, was president, CEO and a charter member of the Lavon Gray Fan Club. She thought I was amazing and could do no wrong, so when I returned home with the certificate, she immediately took a photo and submitted it to our small-town Mississippi newspaper, The *Simpson County News*.

Now here's the deal: since I was the oldest grandchild, I was the first to take piano lessons. Because of this, my family didn't know the highest score possible was a "Superior" and that everyone received an "Excellent." After all, who wants to give an aspiring seven-year old pianist an "Average," forever thwarting their musical ambitions?

A few weeks following the festival I went to the mailbox, a routine I relished as a young boy. To my surprise there was an envelope addressed to: Mr. Lavon Gray. I immediately ran across the country road into my grandmother's un-air-conditioned house, all the time proudly waving the letter and shouting to the top of my lungs, "I got mail! I got mail!"

Gathered around the kitchen bar, with the smell of bacon and eggs still lingering from breakfast, my entire family quickly opened the envelope and pulled out a card emblazoned with the Great Seal of the United States House of Representatives. The card was from our U.S. Congressman, G.V. "Sonny" Montgomery, who represented Mississippi's 4th Congressional District. On the cover of the card was printed the words, "I read something nice about you" and the inside contained the newspaper clipping from the local paper. Of course, Congressman Montgomery didn't actually send the clipping himself. In fact, he probably never saw it. I'm sure an intern clipped the photo from the paper, dropped in a pre-printed card, and mailed it to my address. Nothing amazing about that, right?

WRONG!

You see, my grandmother came from a family of eight children, all of whom lived in rural Simpson County and most within a 3-mile radius of each other on Poplar Springs Road. When spouses and children were counted, there were a total of 127 registered voters in the family. What was more significant is they voted as a block. Every single election. Every single time.

In election years, voting-age members of our family would overflow my grandmother's living room as she walked through the upcoming ballet, race by race, candidate by candidate, identifying who they would support. If they couldn't reach consensus, my grandmother, the matriarch and quasi "Godfather" of the family, would announce the preferred candidate and they would move on. They knew their strength was in unified numbers, so they never wavered from their choices. Never.

My grandmother never met Congressman Montgomery, and I'm relatively sure my family knew little about his role as chairman of the Veteran's Affairs Committee, or that he received the Presidential Medal of Honor. But I can assure you of this: Sonny Montgomery received 127 votes every two years from my family. Not because of the issues he supported or opposed, but because he set in motion a process that honored an insignificant seven-year-old Mississippi boy who received a substandard "Excellent" at a now-forgotten piano festival...*although he never saw the card himself.*

You're probably saying, "That's a great story but it really wasn't that significant." Well, there's more. My grandmother died in 2015 at the age of ninety-five. Following her funeral, my family and I went to her house one final time to sort through items she had left behind. There were no expensive treasures, large bank statements or priceless collectables to sift through. Just simple trinkets from past holidays, photos of her family and a lifetime of memories.

Then I saw it. On the table next to her chair I noticed her bible. It was the same one she had used for the 47 years I had been on this earth, sitting in the same location it always had. As I picked it up and opened it, my eyes immediately filled with tears. Inside that old, worn bible was a card from Congressman G.V. "Sonny" Montgomery emblazoned with the Great Seal of the U.S. House of Representatives. On the cover of the card were printed the words, "I read something nice about you" and the inside contained the newspaper clipping memorializing my piano masterpiece from 1974. *My grandmother kept that card for forty years.*

Your greatest contributions in life won't be the strategic plan you develop or the business you build. Heck, it won't even be the money you earn. At the end of your life, when all is said and done, your greatest impact will be the difference you make in the people around you. The meaningful relationships you forge with even the most difficult personalities. The impact you have in the pigpen.

So, will you spend your life *wrestling with pigs* or *building relationships?* The choice is yours but choose wisely...those of us around you are depending on it!

Figure 2:
Card received from G.V. (Sonny)
Montgomery's Office, c. July 1974

Figure 3:
Newspaper clipping from The
Simpson County News, c. June 1974

WORKS CITED

Aesop, Sixth century B.C. 1909–14. *Aesop's fables, retold by Joseph Jacobs.* New York: P.F. Collier & Son. Accessed June 9, 2019. https://www.bartleby.com/17/1/62.html.

Aurora. 2017. *Butch from The Little Rascals, the Villain I Love to Hate.* April 29. Accessed May 5, 2019. https://aurorasginjoint.com/2017/04/29/butch-from-the-little-rascals-the-villain-i-love-to-hate/.

Chibana, Nayomi. n.d. *Things You Can Do to Stop Passive-Aggressive Behavior in the Workplace.* Accessed June 9, 2019. https://visme.co/blog/passive-aggressive-behaviors-in-the-workplace-infographic/.

CPP, Inc. 2018. *Workplace Conflict and How Businesses Can Harness it to Thrive.* Mountain View, CA: CPP, Inc.

CURNUTTE, MARISSA. 2014. *The Big Problem With Mini-Pigs.* October 1. Accessed April 5, 2019. https://news.nationalgeographic.com/news/2014/09/140930-animals-culture-science-miniature-pigs-breeders-sanctuaries/.

Dallek, Robert. 2005. *Lyndon B. Johnson: The Portrait of a President.* New York: Oxford University Press.

n.d. *Fandom.* Accessed June 9, 2019. https://disney.fandom.com/wiki/Pumbaa.

Gallup. 2018. *State of the American Workforce.* Washington, D.C.: Gallup.

History.com. 2019. *Black Death.* June 6. Accessed August 11, 2019. https://www.history.com/topics/middle-ages/black-death.

Hughes, Sloane. 2019. *Funny or Die.* May 31. Accessed June 8, 2019. https://www.funnyordie.com/2019/5/31/18647832/p

eople-are-mad-that-pumbaa-a-warthog-looks-like-a-warthog-the-lion-king-live-action.

Kane, Sally. 2019. *Workplace Bullying: Facts and Figures.* February 20. Accessed May 5, 2019. https://www.thebalancecareers.com/workplace-bullying-bullying-facts-and-figures-2164325.

Mark Howard Long, Ph. D. 2010-2011. *The Johnson Treatment.* Accessed May 5, 2019. https://sites.google.com/site/ucf2020/sources/student-pages/the-johnson-treatment.

Maxwell, John C. 2005. *Developing the Leaders Around You: How to Help Others Reach Their Full Potential.* Lawrenceville, GA : Nelson Business.

Mayo Clinic. 2017. *Narcissistic Personality Disorder.* 18 November. Accessed August 9, 2019. https://www.mayoclinic.org/diseases-conditions/narcissistic-personality-disorder/symptoms-causes/syc-20366662.

Morris, Chris. 2018. *61 million Gen Zers are about to enter the US workforce and radically change it forever.* May 2. Accessed August 1, 2019. https://www.cnbc.com/2018/05/01/61-million-gen-zers-about-to-enter-us-workforce-and-change-it.html.

National Academy of Sciences. 2018. *Human ectoparasites and the spread of plague in Europe during the Second Pandemic.* Proceedings of the National Academy of Sciences in the United States. https://www.pnas.org/content/115/6/1304.abstract?_ga=2.227485917.172445843.1565572118-1235750267.1563236283.

Nichol, Peter B. 2016. *Narcissistic CEO's Kill Companies: How to Predict How They Will Behave.* September 6. Accessed

August 7, 2019.
https://leadersneedpancakes.com/narcissistic-ceos-kill-companies/.

Okamoto, Yoichi. 1965. *President Lyndon B. Johnson & Abe Fortas, photograph, public domain.* July 29. Accessed August 10, 2019. http://www.lbjlibrary.net/collections/photo-archive.html.

Umoh, Ruth. 2018. *"The CEO of LinkedIn shares the No. 1 job skill American employees are lacking".* April 26. Accessed May 5, 2019. https://www.cnbc.com/2018/04/26/linkedin-ceo-the-no-1-job-skill-american-employees-lack.html.

Wikipedia. 2019. *Charlotte's Web.* August 2. Accessed August 9, 2019.
https://en.wikipedia.org/wiki/Charlotte%27s_Web.

Workplace Bullying Institute. n.d. *The WBI Definition of Workplace Bullying.* Accessed May 5, 2019.
https://www.workplacebullying.org/individuals/problem/definition/.

About the Author

L. Lavon Gray, Ph.D., has spent over three decades investing in leaders across the U.S. and around the world. In addition to his extensive experience as a speaker, executive coach and corporate culture expert, Lavon holds a certification in conflict resolution from Cornell University and has completed professional leadership development through Harvard University. To support his work with corporate and non-profit leaders, Lavon developed the *Workplace Conflict Index®* to assist organizations in identifying their internal conflict levels and develop strategies to promote organization health.

As a veteran sports official, Lavon brings a unique perspective to the field of conflict resolution. He currently works as an on-field NCAA football official and has officiated in numerous collegiate conferences across the East Coast. An award-winning author, he is a professional member of the National Speaker's Association and Forbes Coaches Council and is a certified speaker and leadership coach with The John Maxwell Team.

Bring Lavon Gray to Your Organization!

www.LavonGray.com
www.NeverWrestleWithPigs.com
llg@lavongray.com
601.421.7100

Keynotes

Define Your Tomorrow
A Proven Path to Success

Never Wrestle with Pigs
Dealing with Difficult Personalities

Choose to Defuse
Conflict Resolution in the Battle

Invisible No More
Building High-Impact Relationships

Workshops

After Further Review
Next Level Leadership Skills

Define Your Tomorrow
Skills that Shape Your Success

Mastering the Art of Change
Facilitating Healthy Transformation

Building PowerHouse Teams
High-Impact Collaboration

Selected Forbes Articles

Five Signs Your Work Culture is Toxic
The Dying Art of Building Relationships
Five Guaranteed Ways to Get an "F" as a Leader
Choose to Defuse: Three Keys to Conflict Resolution
When the Crowd Turns: How to Soar When Your Supporters Bail
Keeping Your Cool: Three Keys to Avoiding Workplace Meltdowns
After Further Review: Four Keys for Handling Leadership Errors

What Others are Saying

"Probably one of the most entertaining corporate speakers I've heard."
– BENJAMIN TEAGUE, Vice-President of Strategic Development
Biltmore Farms, LLC – Asheville, North Carolina

"Lavon Gray lives what he believes… convincing, convicting, and contagious."
– DERRIC JOHNSON, Former Creative Consultant
The Walt Disney Company – Orlando, Florida

"Dr. Gray used humor, storytelling, and practical examples that our members could put into practice immediately.
– SHARI T. VEAZEY, Executive Director
Mississippi Municipal League – Jackson, Mississippi

"Lavon is the total package for leadership development and is one of the most effective speakers we've ever used."
– GARY GENTRY, Owner
Premier Productions – Greenville, South Carolina

"Lavon offers a captivating and intuitive perspective at how people communicate when they disagree."
– JERRY BREWER, President
NAIFA Mississippi – Jackson, Mississippi

Lavon's dynamic personality and speaking skills, along with his genuine character, give him the ability to work with anyone. If your organization wants to improve its performance, Lavon Gray can help make that happen."
– HONORABLE RONNIE MUSGROVE
Governor of the State of Mississippi, 1996 – 2000

"Lavon Gray's presentations on leadership are motivating and powerful. He challenged us to take our leadership to the next level."
– ORLANDO EXPERIENCE CONFERENCE